What is Spotty Powder anyway?!

"Spotty Powder!" exclaimed Mr. Wonka, beaming at the company. "There it is! That's it! Fantastic stuff!"

"It looks like sugar," said Miranda Piker.

"It's meant to look like sugar," Mr. Wonka said. "And it tastes like sugar. But it isn't sugar. Oh, dear me, no."

"Then what is it?" asked Miranda Piker, speaking rather rudely.

"That door over there," said Mr. Wonka, turning away from Miranda and pointing to a small red door at the far end of the room, "leads directly down to the machine that makes the powder. Twice a day, I go down there myself to feed it. But I'm the only one. Nobody ever comes with me."

They all stared at the little door on which it said MOST SECRET—KEEP OUT.

Puffin Books by Roald Dahl

ROALD DAHL

The MISSING GOLDEN
Ticket
AND OTHER SPLENDIFEROUS SECRETS

ILLUSTRATED BY QUENTIN BLAKE

PUFFIN BOOKS
An Imprint of Penguin Group (USA) Inc.

Find out more about Roald Dahl
by visiting the website at
roalddahl.com

PUFFIN BOOKS
Published by the Penguin Group
Penguin Young Readers Group, 345 Hudson Street, New York, New York 10014, U.S.A.
Penguin Group (Canada), 90 Eglinton Avenue East, Suite 700, Toronto, Ontario M4P 2Y3, Canada
(a division of Pearson Penguin Canada Inc.)
Penguin Books Ltd, 80 Strand, London WC2R 0RL, England
Penguin Ireland, 25 St Stephen's Green, Dublin 2, Ireland (a division of Penguin Books Ltd)
Penguin Group (Australia), 707 Collins St., Melbourne, Victoria 3008, Australia
(a division of Pearson Australia Group Pty Ltd)
Penguin Books India Pvt Ltd, 11 Community Centre, Panchsheel Park, New Delhi–110 017, India
Penguin Group (NZ), 67 Apollo Drive, Rosedale, Auckland 0632, New Zealand
(a division of Pearson New Zealand Ltd)
Penguin Books, Rosebank Office Park, 181 Jan Smuts Avenue, Parktown North 2193, South Africa
Penguin China, B7 Jaiming Center, 27 East Third Ring Road North,
Chaoyang District, Beijing 100020, China

Penguin Books Ltd, Registered Offices: 80 Strand, London WC2R 0RL, England

First published in Great Britain by Penguin Books Ltd, 2010
First published in the United States of America by Puffin Books, 2010
Reissued in this edition by Puffin Books, an imprint of Penguin Young Readers Group, 2013

9 10 8

Text and archive photographs copyright © Road Dahl Nominee Ltd, 2010
Illustrations copyright © Quentin Blake, 2010
All rights reserved

Extracts taken from: *The Roald Dahl Diary 1992*, first published 1991; *Charlie's Secret Chocolate
Box*, first published 1997; *D is for Dahl*, first published 2004; *The Dahlmanac*, first published 2006;
Dahlmanac 2, first published 2007; *More About Boy*, first published 2008—all published in Puffin
Books; *Roald Dahl's Cookbook*, published by Penguin Books 1996; "Spotty Powder," first published
in *Puffin Post*, Vol. 7, No. 1, 1973; "Strawberry-flavored Chocolate-coated Fudge" and "Butterscotch"
from *Roald Dahl's Revolting Recipes*, published by Jonathan Cape Ltd 1994.

LIBRARY OF CONGRESS CATALOGING-IN-PUBLICATION DATA
Dahl, Roald
The missing golden ticket and other splendiferous secrets / Roald Dahl ; illustrated by Quentin
Blake.
p. cm.
ISBN 978-0-14-241742-3 (pbk.)
1. Dahl, Roald—Juvenile literature.
2. Authors, English—20th century—Biography—Juvenile literature.
I. Blake, Quentin, ill. II. Title.
PR6054.A35Z467 2010
823'.914—dc22
[B]
2010021712

Text design by Dan Newman
Set in Adobe Caslon Pro and Filosofia

Printed in the United States of America

ALWAYS LEARNING   PEARSON

Roald Dahl loved secrets.

This was his advice from *The Minpins*: "Above all, watch with glittering eyes the whole world around you because the greatest secrets are always hidden in the most likely places. Those who don't believe in magic will never find it."

Did you know...

✳ Augustus Gloop was originally named Augustus Pottle?

✳ *Willy Wonka's Oompa-Loompas were going to be called Whipple-Scrumpets?*

✳ Cocoa pods are as big as rugby balls.

✳ *Roald Dahl wanted to get rid of history teachers and have chocolate teachers instead.*

These are just some of the splendiferous secrets you'll discover in this delicious little treasure trove of Roald Dahl fun facts and surprises. You'll also meet Quentin Blake, find out how to make strawberry-flavored chocolate-coated fudge (YUM!), sneak a peek at Roald Dahl's school reports and much, much more.

How Roald Dahl started writing Charlie and the Chocolate Factory

"*Charlie and the Chocolate Factory* took me a terrible long time to write. The first time I did it, I got everything wrong. I wrote a story about a little boy who was going round a chocolate factory and he accidentally fell into a big tub of melted chocolate and got sucked into the machine that made chocolate figures and he couldn't get out. It was a splendid big chocolate figure, a chocolate boy the same size as him. And it was Easter time, and the figure was put in a shop window, and in the end a lady came in and bought it as an Easter present for her little girl, and carried it home. On Easter Day, the little girl opened the box with her present in it, and took it out and then she decided to eat some of it. She would start with the head, she thought. So she broke off the nose, and when she saw a real human nose sticking out underneath and two big bright human eyes staring at

her through the eye-holes in the chocolate, she got a nasty shock. And so it went on.

"But the story wasn't good enough. I rewrote it, and rewrote it, and the little tentacles kept shooting out from my

Mike Teavee

2

head, searching for new ideas, and at last one of them came back with Mr. Willy Wonka and his marvelous chocolate factory and then came Charlie and his parents and grandparents and the Golden Tickets and the nasty children, Violet Beauregarde and Veruca Salt and all the rest of them.

Violet
Beauregarde

"As a matter of fact, I got so wrapped up in all those nasty children, and they made me giggle so much that I couldn't stop inventing them. In the first full version of *Charlie and the Chocolate Factory*, I had no less than ten horrid little boys and girls. That was too many. It became confusing. It wasn't a good book. But I liked

them all so much, I didn't want to take any
of them out.

"One of them, who was taken out in
the end, was a horrid little girl who was
disgustingly rude to her parents and also
thoroughly disobedient. Her name was
Miranda Mary Piker . . ."

Who was
Miranda Mary Piker?
Find out later in
this book!

Roald Dahl's Year

Nature is full of secrets if you look hard enough. And Roald Dahl kept notes about the habits of butterflies and frogs, the color and songs of birds, and the different flowers, plants and berries that blossomed in the countryside. Find out what Roald Dahl liked or disliked about every month of the year, including his favorite animals and birds. (And read about some of the hilarious pranks he got up to when he was a young boy too!)

Roald Dahl's January

❝ For the last twelve months we have all been living in one year and now all of a sudden it is another. It is extraordinary how this tremendous change takes place in the space of a fraction of a second. As the clock approaches midnight on the thirty-first of December you are still in the old year, but then all at once, one millionth of a second after midnight, you are in the new. I have always found this sudden change from one year to another awfully hard to get used to, and all through the new January that follows I keep writing down the old year instead of the new one on letters and other bits of paper . . .

"There is just one small bright spark shining through the gloom in my January garden. The first snowdrops are in flower. "

The Missing Children

As you now know, Roald Dahl wrote several versions of *Charlie and the Chocolate Factory* and included lots of very naughty characters. In a very early draft of the story, as many as *ten* children are lucky Golden Ticket finders who each win a tour of Mr. Wonka's Chocolate Factory:

Augustus Pottle who falls in the chocolate river
Miranda Grope who also falls in after him

Wilbur Rice and Tommy Troutbeck
who climb in wagons running from the
vanilla fudge mountain and end up in
the Pounding and Cutting Room

Violet Strabismus who turns purple
after chewing the three-course-meal gum

Clarence Crump, Bertie Upside and
Terence Roper who each cram a whole
mouthful of warming candies and end
up overheating

Elvira Entwhistle who falls foul of
the squirrels in the Nut Room

And Charlie Bucket who gets stuck
inside a chocolate statue and witnesses
a burglary—and receives a very unusual
reward . . .

Roald Dahl soon decided there were too many naughty children in the story. So, somewhat reluctantly, he reduced the number of lucky Golden Ticket finders to seven, and gave all the children distinct characteristics:

Charlie Bucket

A nice boy

Augustus Gloop

(previously Augustus Pottle)
A greedy boy

Marvin Prune

A conceited boy
(we never find out
what happens to him)

Herpes Trout

A television-crazy boy
(he became Mike Teavee
in the final version!)

Veruca Salt

A girl who
is allowed
to HAVE
anything she
wants

A girl who
chews gum all
day long

Violet Beauregarde

And one more . . .

Miranda Mary Piker

A girl who is allowed to DO anything she wants

And it is in this draft that Charlie's grandparents are introduced for the first time, and tiny people called "Whipple-Scrumpets" become Mr. Wonka's workforce, reciting poems as each child leaves.

Chocolate!
Everything you always wanted to know

The Swiss eat more chocolate per person than any other nation in the world.

Belgium is the third biggest producer of chocolate in the world.

Just like Willy Wonka, many Belgian chocolate makers keep their recipes secret.

*Cocoa was discovered by the South
American Indians over 3,000 years ago.*

The word "chocolate" comes from *chocolatl*,
the Aztec name for their chocolate drink.

The scientific name for cocoa
means **"food of the gods."**

Cocoa beans were considered so valuable,
the Aztecs used them as money – ten beans
would buy a rabbit!

Originally, chocolate was used just as a drink. The Spaniards took cocoa to Europe from Mexico in the sixteenth century.

They kept the recipe for drinking-chocolate secret for nearly 100 years!

In 1606, an Italian took the recipe to Italy, and chocolate drinking became popular throughout Europe.

There was a **royal chocolate maker** at the court of Louis XIV.

At first, chocolate was only for the rich. They drank it in "chocolate houses," which were like cafes.

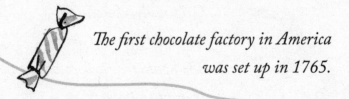

The first chocolate factory in America was set up in 1765.

Cocoa powder is made from dried beans that are roasted and ground.

It takes a year's crop of cocoa beans from one tree to make just one tin of cocoa!

Cocoa pods are as big as rugby balls. They contain about thirty beans.

Factories can produce over **five million bars** of chocolate a day.

Roald Dahl's February

"Only once have I discovered a new molehill in our orchard in the month of February. I love seeing molehills because they tell me that only a few inches below the surface some charming and harmless little fellow is living his own private busy life scurrying up and down his tunnels hunting for food . . .

"Do you know anything about moles? They are remarkable animals. They are shy and gentle and their fur coats are softer than

velvet. They are so shy that you will seldom see one on the surface . . . The molehills that you see are not of course their houses.

They are simply piles of loose soil that a mole has pushed up out of the way because, after all, if you are digging an underground tunnel you have to put the excavated soil somewhere.

"His food consists of worms, leather-jackets, centipedes and beetle grubs, and the fantastic thing is that he actually has to eat *one half of his own body weight* of these tiny delicacies every single day in order to stay alive! No wonder he's a busy fellow. Just imagine how much food *you* would have to eat to consume half your own body weight! Fifty hamburgers, one hundred loaves of bread and a bucketful of Mars Bars *and* the rest of it each and every day. It makes one quite ill to think about it! "

The Whipple-Scrumpets

Have a look at an early version of the Whipple-Scrumpets' song about greedy Augustus Gloop, and compare it to the one that actually appears in *Charlie and the Chocolate Factory*, sung by the Oompa-Loompas. Can you spot the differences?

The Whipple-Scrumpets ... began dancing about and clapping their hands and singing:

"Augustus Gloop! Augustus Gloop!
The great big greedy nincompoop!

How long could we allow this beast
To gorge and guzzle, feed and feast
On everything he wanted to?
Great Scott! It simply wouldn't do!
And so, you see, the time was ripe
To send him shooting up the pipe;
He had to go. It had to be.
And very soon he's going to see
Inside the room to which he's gone
Some funny things are going on.

But don't, dear children, be alarmed.
Augustus Gloop will not be harmed,
Although, of course, we must admit
He will be altered quite a bit.
For instance, all those lumps of fat
Will disappear just like that!
He'll shrink and shrink and shrink and shrink,
His skin will be no longer pink,
He'll be so smooth and square and small
He will not know himself at all.
Farewell, Augustus Gloop, farewell!
For soon you'll be a caramel!"

"They're teasing," Mr. Wonka said, shaking a finger at the singing Whipple-Scrumpets. "You mustn't believe a word they say."

Mr. Wonka's Chocolate Factory Recipes

Strawberry-flavored Chocolate-coated Fudge

You will need:

9 x 9 in. shallow baking pan

Waxed paper

Large saucepan

Sugar thermometer

Cookie cutters

1 lb. sugar

½ cup unsalted butter

¾ cup evaporated milk

A few generous drops of pink food coloring

A generous ½ tsp of strawberry food flavoring

½ cup melted chocolate for dipping

Makes enough for ten greedy children

How to make:

 1 Line the pan with buttered waxed paper.

 2 Put all the ingredients except the flavoring and coloring into a large heavy-bottomed saucepan and place over a low heat.

 3 Stir occasionally. Once the sugar has dissolved, gently boil the mixture and now stir all the time (to prevent sticking and burning on the bottom of the pan).

4 Place the sugar thermometer into the saucepan and boil the mixture to a soft ball (about 244°F). This takes about five minutes.

5 Take the pan off the heat, stir until the bubbles subside and then add the flavoring and the coloring.

 6 Beat rapidly with a wooden spoon until the mixture thickens and becomes granular, approximately three minutes.

 7 Pour the fudge into the lined pan and leave to set. If necessary, smooth with a palette knife dipped into boiling water.

8 With cookie cutters, cut out the fudge and dip one side into the melted chocolate, or decorate with piped chocolate, creating different patterns.

Please ask a grown-up to help you when you are handling anything hot.

Roald Dahl's Favorite Things

Come rain, shine, frost or snow,
Roald Dahl could be found inside the
shed at the end of his garden.
This was where he wrote.
And beside him there
was a table where
he kept his most
favorite things.
They're all still there.

Here are some of the items on Roald Dahl's table:

1. A ball made from silver chocolate wrappers.
2. A small model of a Hurricane fighter plane.
3. His hipbone.
4. A glass bottle filled with mauve-colored bits of gristle taken from Roald Dahl's spine during an operation.
5. A photo of his granddaughter Sophie.
6. A meteorite the size of a golf ball.
7. His father's silver-and-tortoiseshell paper-knife.
8. A solar-powered musical box.
9. A carving of a green grasshopper.
10. A cone from a cedar tree.

Roald Dahl's March

"I rather like the month of March . . . your heart is lifted by the signs of approaching spring all around you. Halfway through the month most of the hedges are covered with a pale powdering of green as the little leaf buds begin to burst, and the pussy willows are smothered in yellow pollen. Crocuses are flowering brilliantly and best of all, the nesting season is beginning to get seriously under way . . . I can see a pair of blackbirds

building high up in the trunk of the big
clipped yew tree . . . I watch a thrush carrying
bits of dry grass up into the branches of the
vine . . . I see a pair of blue chickadees
popping in and out of a small hole in the
wooden tool shed . . . I see a pair of robins
making a mossy nest in the bank underneath
the heather bed . . .

"By the end of the month ladybugs are on the wing once again, and you will notice that nearly all of them are the two-spotted kind. Peacock butterflies and small tortoiseshells are emerging from their winter sleep, hunting for early flowers. Bumblebees and honeybees have also woken up and are in among the crocuses, looking for pollen. "

Meet
Quentin Blake

Roald Dahl and Quentin Blake make
a perfect partnership of words and
illustrations, but when Roald started
writing, he had many different illustrators.
Quentin started working with
him in 1976 (the first
book he illustrated was
The Enormous Crocodile,
published in 1978)
and from then
on they worked

together until Roald's death. Quentin
ended up illustrating all of Roald Dahl's
books, with the exception of *The Minpins*.

To begin with, Quentin was a bit nervous
about working with such a very famous
author, but by the time they collaborated
on *The BFG*, they had become firm friends.
Quentin never knew anything about a new

story until the manuscript arrived. "You'll have some fun with this," Roald would say – or, "You'll have some trouble with this." Quentin would make lots of rough drawings to take along to Gipsy House, where he would show them to Roald and see what he thought. Roald Dahl liked his books to be packed with illustrations – Quentin ended up drawing twice as many pictures for *The BFG* as he had originally been asked for.

Quentin Blake was born on December 16, 1932. His first drawing was published when he was sixteen, and he has written and illustrated many of his own books, as well as Roald Dahl's. Besides being an illustrator he taught for over twenty years at the Royal College of Art – he is a real professor!

What Roald Dahl thought of Quentin Blake

"It is Quent's pictures rather than my own written descriptions that have brought to life such characters as the BFG, Miss Trunchbull, Mr. Twit and The Grand High Witch. It is the faces and the bodies he draws that are remembered by children all over the world . . . When he and I work together on a new book and he has a pen in his hand, it is magical to watch the facility with which he can sketch out a

character or
a scene. 'You mean
more like this?' he will say,
and the nib will fly over the paper at
incredible speed, making thin lines in
black ink, and in thirty seconds he has
produced a new picture. 'Perhaps,' I will
say, 'he should have a more threatening look
about him.' Once again the pen flies over
the paper and there before you is exactly
what you are after. But this is not to say that
I 'help' him with many of the characters he
draws for my books. Most of them he does
entirely on his own and they are far better
and funnier than anything I could think of. "

Ideas Books

Roald Dahl kept two ideas books for about forty years. They were both old school exercise books, the first of which was sandy colored, and the second red and very battered. He thought that good ideas were like dreams – soon forgotten – and made sure that he wrote them down straight away. He then ticked the really good ideas and crossed out the ones he had used. Some ideas were developed years and years after they were jotted down. Can you guess which books came from these ideas?

A story about Mr. Fox who has a whole network of underground tunnels leading to all the shops in the village. At night, he goes up through the floorboards and helps himself.

What about a chocolate factory that makes fantastic and marvellous things — with a crazy man running it?

If Roald Dahl hadn't been an author, he could have been a doctor, a boxer, a golfer, an inventor, a scientist, a botanist or a picture framer. He had a natural talent for all of these things. And he was interested in just

Ideas for *Fantastic Mr. Fox* and *Charlie and the Chocolate Factory*

about EVERYTHING. But here are a
few of the things he was especially
fascinated by:

Nineteenth- and twentieth-century paintings

Eighteenth-century English furniture

Gardening

Orchids

Music

Wine

Gambling

Good food

Chocolate

Roald Dahl once said, "If I were a
headmaster I would get rid of the history
teacher and get a chocolate teacher instead."

Roald Dahl's April

❝Now at last we can say that spring has arrived, and with it come flocks of summer migrants, all those little birds that flew away to the warmer countries in the south when it began to get cold last October. Most of them go as far as North Africa and don't ask me how they find their way there and back again because that is one of the great mysteries of the world. There are skylarks, greenfinches, goldfinches, whitethroats, willow-warblers,

golden plovers, blackcaps, swallows, house-
martins, chiffchaffs and many more besides,
and soon after they arrive they pair up and
start to build their nests. "

Roald Dahl's School Reports

In 1929, when he was thirteen, Roald Dahl was sent to boarding school. You would expect him to get wonderful marks in English – but his school reports were not good!

EASTER TERM, aged 15. *English Composition.* "A persistent muddler. Vocabulary negligible, sentences malconstructed. He reminds me of a camel."

SUMMER TERM, aged 16. *English Composition.* "This boy is an indolent and illiterate member of the class."

There's worse to come!

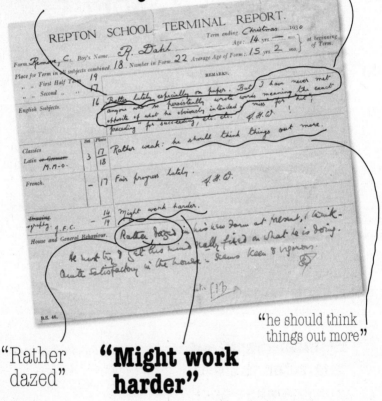

"**Better lately**"

"I never met anyone who so persistently wrote words meaning the exact opposite of what he obviously intended"

"he should think things out more"

"Rather dazed"

"**Might work harder**"

"ideas limited"

"Consistently idle: too pleased with himself"

REPTON SCHOOL TERMINAL REPORT.

Form R² Boy's Name R. Dahl Term ending July 26 1932

Place for Term in all subjects combined 12 Number in Form 12 Average Age of Form: 16 yrs. 9 mo. } at beginning of Term

" " First Half Term 12 Age: 15 yrs. 7 mo.

" " Second " 12

English Subjects. REMARKS.

Hist. 6. Has done better this term: his work has sometimes been really good. R.B.

Engl. Satisfactory work: ideas limited. R²B

Scrip. Consistently idle: too pleased with himself. H.S.

Classics Set Place

Latin or German. II Satisfactory progress for me. W.W.

French. 12 During the 2nd half term he has produced better work. These little doubt but he often tries to hide idleness behind a veil of stupidity. His own growth may perhaps excuse some of his apathy. S.F.

Drawing.

House and General Behaviour. He is so large that it is often difficult to remember how young he is. It is time however that he put more effort into his work: he is capable of doing quite respectable work.

B.S. 46. At the least he could produce by a good way.

"He is so large that it is often difficult to remember how young he is"

"he often tries to hide idleness behind a veil of stupidity . . ."

Roald Dahl's May

"May is the month of the cuckoo...
Everyone living in the countryside knows
when the cuckoos start arriving because you
cannot help hearing the loud, eerie, almost
human call of the male bird. It quite literally
says, 'Cuck-koo, cuck-koo,' and the voice
carries for miles... Unlike most other birds,
cuckoos do not pair up and stay together,
so there are no marriages or family life in
cuckooland. No cuckoo has ever bothered to

build its own nest or hatch or feed its young.
The female (carrying her egg in her beak)
searches the hedgerows until she finds the
nest of another bird that already has eggs
in it, and she slips her own egg in with the

others and flies away and forgets all about it.

" . . . The mother hedge sparrow doesn't
seem to mind at all and proceeds to sit on
the egg and incubate it together with her
own. Little does she know what is going
to happen when all the eggs hatch . . . the
cuckoo chick grows three times as fast as the
little sparrows. The overgrown baby cuckoo
proceeds quite literally to push the baby
hedge sparrows one by one out of the nest
to die, and in the end all that is left is this
grotesque, huge, fluffy cuckoo chick filling
the entire nest. The hedge sparrow parents
don't seem to notice what has happened
and they go on feeding this murderer until
in the end it is big enough to hop out of
the nest and fly away without so much
as a thank you! "

Roald's Family Holidays

SPRING

Roald Dahl's father died when Roald was only three so his mother brought up him and his sisters on her own.

Every Easter she rented a house in Tenby, Wales, and took all the children there for a holiday.

The house, called The Cabin, was right next to the sea. When the tide was in, the waves broke right up against one wall of the house. Roald and his sisters used to collect winkles and eat them on slices of bread and butter.

Roald Dahl's
June

"June is the month of the foxglove,
perhaps the most beautiful of all the wild
flowers. The foxglove also gives us a drug
called digitalis which is valuable to doctors
in treating heart conditions. Barley is already
standing tall in the fields. Don't confuse it
with the other two main cereals, wheat and
oats. Barley has long itchy spikes covering the
seeds, and if you pick one of these heads and
slip it under the sleeve of your jacket or shirt

with the long spikes pointing downwards, the head will actually climb all the way up to your shoulder as you walk along swinging your arm.

"During this month the tadpoles in the ponds are beginning to sprout tiny arms and legs, and soon they will be turning into small frogs. Be nice to frogs, by the way. They are your friends in the garden. They eat the beastly slugs and never harm your flowers.

There is so much beauty in the countryside
in June. The lovely pink dog roses are
in full bloom along the hedges and wild
honeysuckle is plentiful.

"I'm afraid that if you live in a town you
don't see any of these splendid sights . . ."

A Missing Chapter

The following secret chapter was originally included in *Charlie and the Chocolate Factory*. But because there were too many naughty children in the earlier versions of the book, "Spotty Powder" – and the revolting Miranda Mary Piker – had to be dropped.

Luckily, Roald Dahl kept it in a very safe place, so you could read it here . . .

Spotty Powder

"This stuff," said Mr. Wonka, "is going to
cause chaos in schools all over the world
when I get it in the shops."

The room they now entered had rows and
rows of pipes coming straight up out of the
floor. The pipes were bent over at the top
and they looked like large walking sticks.
Out of every pipe there trickled a stream
of white crystals. Hundreds of Oompa-
Loompas were running to and fro, catching

the crystals in little golden boxes and stacking the boxes against the walls.

"Spotty Powder!" exclaimed Mr. Wonka, beaming at the company. "There it is! That's it! Fantastic stuff!"

"It looks like sugar," said Miranda Piker.

"It's meant to look like sugar," Mr. Wonka said. "And it tastes like sugar. But it isn't sugar. Oh, dear me, no."

"Then what is it?" asked Miranda Piker, speaking rather rudely.

"That door over there," said Mr. Wonka, turning away from Miranda and pointing to a small red door at the far end of the room, "leads directly down to the machine that makes the powder. Twice a day, I go down there myself to feed it. But I'm the only one. Nobody ever comes with me."

They all stared at the little door on which it said MOST SECRET – KEEP OUT.

The hum and throb of powerful machinery could be heard coming up from the depths below, and the floor itself was vibrating all the time. The children could feel it through the soles of their shoes.

Miranda Piker now pushed forward and stood in front of Mr. Wonka. She was a nasty-looking girl with a smug face and a smirk on her mouth, and whenever she spoke it was always with a voice that seemed to be saying, "Everybody is a fool except me."

"OK," Miranda Piker said, smirking at Mr. Wonka. "So what's the big news? What's this stuff meant to do when you eat it?"

"Ah-ha," said Mr. Wonka, his eyes sparkling with glee. "You'd never guess that, not in a million years. Now listen. All you have to do is sprinkle it over your cereal at breakfast-time, pretending it's sugar. Then you eat it. And then, exactly five seconds after that, you come out in bright red spots all over your face and neck."

"What sort of a silly twit wants spots on his face at breakfast-time?" said Miranda Piker.

"Let me finish," said Mr. Wonka. "So then your mother looks at you across the table and says, 'My poor child. You must have chickenpox. You can't possibly go to school today.' So you stay at home. But by lunch-time, the spots have all disappeared."

"Terrific!" shouted Charlie. "That's just what I want for the day we have exams!"

"That is the ideal time to use it," said Mr. Wonka. "But you mustn't do it too often or it'll give the game away. Keep it for the really nasty days."

"Father!" cried Miranda Piker. "Did you hear what this stuff does? It's shocking! It mustn't be allowed!"

Mr. Piker, Miranda's father, stepped forward and faced Mr. Wonka. He had a smooth white face like a boiled onion.

"Now see here, Wonka," he said. "I happen to be the headmaster of a large school, and I won't allow you to sell this rubbish to the children! It's . . . criminal! Why, you'll ruin the school system of the entire country!"

"I hope so," said Mr. Wonka.

"It's got to be stopped!" shouted Mr. Piker, waving his cane.

"Who's going to stop it?" asked Mr. Wonka. "In my factory, I make things to please children. I don't care about grown-ups."

"I am top of my form," Miranda Piker said, smirking at Mr. Wonka. "And I've never missed a day's school in my life."

"Then it's time you did," Mr. Wonka said.

"How dare you!" said Mr. Piker.

"All holidays and vacations should be stopped!" cried Miranda. "Children are meant to work, not play."

"Quite right, my girl," cried Mr. Piker, patting Miranda on the top of the head. "All work and no play has made you what you are today."

"Isn't she wonderful?" said Mrs. Piker, beaming at her daughter.

"Come on then, Father!" cried Miranda. "Let's go down into the cellar and smash the machine that makes this dreadful stuff!"

"Forward!" shouted Mr. Piker, brandishing his cane and making a dash for the little red door on which it said MOST SECRET – KEEP OUT.

"Stop!" said Mr. Wonka. "Don't go in there! It's terribly secret!"

"Let's see you stop us, you old goat!" shouted Miranda.

"We'll smash it to smithereens!" yelled Mr. Piker. And a few seconds later the two of them had disappeared through the door.

There was a moment's silence.

Then, far off in the distance, from

somewhere deep underground, there came a fearful scream.

"That's my husband!" cried Mrs. Piker, going blue in the face.

There was another scream.

"And that's Miranda!" yelled Mrs. Piker, beginning to hop around in circles. "What's happening to them? What have you got down there, you dreadful beast?"

"Oh nothing much," Mr. Wonka answered. "Just a lot of cogs and wheels and chains and things like that, all going round and round and round."

"You villain!" she screamed. "I know your tricks! You're grinding them into powder! In two minutes my darling Miranda will come pouring out of one of those dreadful pipes, and so will my husband!"

"Of course," said Mr. Wonka. "That's part of the recipe."

"It's what!"

"We've got to use one or two schoolmasters occasionally or it wouldn't work."

"Did you hear him?" shrieked Mrs. Piker, turning to the others. "He admits it! He's nothing but a cold-blooded murderer!"

Mr. Wonka smiled and patted Mrs. Piker gently on the arm.

"Dear lady," he said, "I was only joking."

"Then why did they scream?" snapped Mrs. Piker. "I distinctly heard them scream!"

"Those weren't screams," Mr. Wonka said. "They were laughs."

"My husband never laughs," said Mrs. Piker.

Mr. Wonka flicked his fingers, and up came an Oompa-Loompa.

"Kindly escort Mrs. Piker to the boiler room," Mr. Wonka said. "Don't fret, dear lady," he went on, shaking Mrs. Piker warmly by the hand. "They'll all come out in the wash. There's nothing to worry about. Off you go. Thank you for coming!

Farewell! Goodbye! A pleasure to meet you!"

"Listen, Charlie!" said Grandpa Joe. "The Oompa-Loompas are starting to sing again!"

"Oh, Miranda Mary Piker!" sang the five Oompa-Loompas, dancing about and laughing and beating madly on their tiny drums.

"Oh, Miranda Mary Piker,
How could anybody like her,
Such a priggish and revolting little kid.
So we said, 'Why don't we fix her
In the Spotty-Powder mixer
Then we're bound to like her better than
*   we did.'*

Soon this child who is so vicious
Will have gotten quite delicious,
And her classmates will have surely
    understood
That instead of saying, 'Miranda!
Oh, the beast! We cannot stand her!'
They'll be saying, 'Oh, how useful
And how good!'"

Roald Dahl's
July

" Sunday afternoons were the only times
we had free throughout the school week,
and most boys went for long walks in the
countryside. But I took no long Sunday
afternoon walks during my last term.
My walks took me only as far as the garage in
Wilmington where my lovely motorbike was
hidden. There I would put on my disguise –
my waders and helmet and goggles and wind
jacket – and go sailing in a state of absolute
bliss through the highways and byways of
Derbyshire. But the greatest thrill of all was

to ride at least once every Sunday afternoon
slap through the middle of Repton village,
sailing past the pompous prefects and the

masters in their gowns and mortarboards.
. . . Don't forget that those were the days
when schools like mine were merciless
places where serious misdemeanours were
punished by savage beatings that drew blood
from your backside. I am quite sure that if I
had ever been caught, that same headmaster
would have thrashed me within an inch of
my life and would probably have expelled
me into the bargain. That is what made it
so exciting. I never told anyone, not even
my best friend, where I went on my Sunday
walks. I had learnt from a tender age that
there are no secrets unless you keep them
to yourself and this was the greatest secret
I had ever had to keep in my life so far. "

What Roald Dahl thought about chocolate

"My passion for chocolate did not really begin until I was fourteen or fifteen years old, and there was a good reason for this. Today chocolate-guzzling begins when the child is about five and it goes on with increasing intensity until the guzzler gets to be about twelve . . .

"Things were different when I was young. The reason that neither I nor any of my generation developed the chocolate-guzzling bug early on was quite simply that in those days there were very few delicious chocolate bars available in the sweet-shops to tempt us. That's why they were called sweet-shops and not chocolate-shops. Had I been born ten years later, it would have been another story, but, unfortunately for me, I grew up in the 1920s and the great golden years of the chocolate revolution had not yet begun.

 "When I was young, a small child going into the sweet-shop clutching his pocket money would be offered very little choice in the way of chocolate bars as we know them today. There was the Cadbury's Bournville Bar and the Dairy Milk Bar. There was the Dairy Milk

Flake (the only great invention so far) and the Whipped-cream Walnut . . . meagre pickings when you compare it with the splendid array of different chocolate bars that you see on display today.

"Consequently, in those days we small boys and girls were much more inclined to spend our money either on sweets and toffees or on some of the many very cheap and fairly disgusting things . . . sherbet-suckers and gobstoppers and liquorice bootlaces and aniseed balls, and we did not mind that the liquorice was made from rat's blood and the sherbet from sawdust. They were cheap and to us they tasted good. So on the whole, we made do with eating sweets and toffees and junk instead of chocolate.

"Then came the revolution and the entire world of chocolate was suddenly turned upside-down in the space of seven glorious years between 1930 and 1937. Here's a brief summary of what happened.

1905 Cadbury's began production of milk-bars, starting with the *Dairy Milk Bar*.

1910 The plain one, the *Bournville Bar*, came five years later.

1920 Then came the first great speciality chocolate bar, the *Dairy Milk Flake*. This was a milestone, the first time any manufacturer had started seriously playing around with chocolate in their Inventing Rooms.

1921 Cadbury's *Fruit and Nut* bar appeared on the market.

1930 A chocolate manufacturing company called Frys invented the *Crunchie*.

1932 Suddenly, a new company appeared called Mars. A young American man called Forrest Mars came to England and in a small laboratory in Slough he started experimenting with his father's recipe for the *Milky Way* to make it better . . . and the *Mars Bar* was born . . . and very soon 600 million of them were being eaten every year in England alone.

1933   Black Magic assorted chocolates
       appeared in boxes.

1935   The lovely Aero was introduced.

1936   Don't forget Forrest Mars. In spite
       of the phenomenal success of his
       Mars Bar, this genius was still
       experimenting in his laboratory and
       came up with another classic beauty –
       Maltesers. In the same year,
       Quality Street was also
       put on to the market.

1937   Another golden year
       during which monumental classic
       lines were invented: Kit Kat, Rolo
       and Smarties."

And – for all you chocolate-guzzlers –
they are all still available in the shops today!

Weird and wonderful Roald Dahl facts

He was very tall – six feet five and three-quarter inches, or nearly two meters. His nickname in the RAF was Lofty, while Walt Disney called him Stalky (because he was like a beanstalk!).

——— ✳ ———

He was a terrible speller, but he liked playing **Scrabble**.

His nickname at home was the Apple, because he was the apple of his mother's eye (which means her favorite!).

———— ✳ ————

He pretended to have appendicitis when he was nine because he was so homesick in his first two weeks at boarding school. He fooled the matron and the school doctor and was sent home. But he couldn't fool his own doctor, who made him promise never to do it again.

———— ✳ ————

He didn't like **cats** – but he did like dogs, birds and goats.

———— ✳ ————

Roald Dahl wrote the screenplay for the James Bond film *You Only Live Twice*.

He once had a
tame magpie.

———— ✳ ————

He was a keen photographer at school
and, when he was eighteen, won two
prizes: one from the Royal Photographic
Society in London and another from the
Photographic
Society of
Holland.

———— ✳ ————

In the churchyard at Great
Missenden, Buckinghamshire,
big friendly giant footprints
lead to Roald Dahl's grave.

Roald's Family Holidays

SUMMER

Best of all were the summer holidays. From the time he was four years old to when he was seventeen, Roald and his family went to Norway every summer. There were no commercial airplanes in those days, so the journey was a splendid expedition. It took four days to get there, and four days to get back again! The sea crossing from Newcastle to Oslo lasted two days and a

night – and Roald was generally seasick.

Finally, they would reach what Roald Dahl called "the magic island," the island of Tjøme in a Norwegian fjord. The family would swim and sunbathe, mess about in rock pools, and go fishing. When Roald was seven, his mother acquired a motor boat and they could explore other islands.

"We would cling to the sides of our funny little white motor boat, driving through mountainous white-capped waves and getting drenched to the skin, while my mother calmly handled the tiller. There were times, I promise you, when the waves were so high that as we slid down into a trough the whole world disappeared from sight . . . It requires great skill to handle a small boat in seas like these . . . But my mother knew exactly how to do it, and we were never afraid."

Roald Dahl's August

"I find August in England a rather torpid month. The trees and plants have all done their growing for the year and nature is hanging motionless in suspension before sinking slowly into the decline of winter. There is a brownish look to the countryside and the leaves are hanging heavy on the trees. But if it is nothing else, it is the month of the butterfly. Butterflies are lovely things. They do no harm to man himself either by

stinging, biting or spreading disease.
Nor are they beneficial to man as the
silkworm is or the honeybee. The large
white or cabbage butterfly is the only one
that is a nuisance because it lays eggs on
your cabbages and these hatch out into
horrid hungry caterpillars . . .

"August is, by the way, the month
when young adders are born in heathy,
hilly places, and baby grass snakes emerge
from their eggs in rotting leaves and old
compost heaps. It is the month when
hedgehogs have their litters of babies,
all born blind and helpless, and I'm afraid
it is also the month when wasps come
on the warpath, stinging humans in
great numbers."

More things that Roald Dahl liked

* Music by
  Beethoven

* **Football**

* Racing greyhounds

* **The color yellow**

* **Conkers**

* **Medical inventions**

* **Rugby**

* Onions

* Breeding homing budgies

* **Golf**

* **The smell of bacon frying**

Advice from Roald Dahl

"At the age of eight I became a mad diary enthusiast . . . I was a bit of a loner in those days and a bit of a dreamer and some of the things I wrote down for the next five or six years were thoughts that I don't think I would have dared even to speak out aloud to myself. That's the beauty of writing. You find that you can actually write things down that are quite outlandish and outrageous and you feel all the better for it."

"I have a passion for teaching kids to become readers, to become comfortable with a book, not daunted. Books shouldn't be daunting, they should be funny, exciting and wonderful; and learning to be a reader gives a terrific advantage."

Roald Dahl's September

❝ I have always loved this month. As a schoolboy I loved it because it is the Month of the Conker . . . We all know, of course, that a great conker is one that has been sorted in a dry place for at least a year. This matures it and makes it rock hard and therefore very formidable. We also know about the short cuts that less dedicated players take to harden their conkers. Some soak them in vinegar for a week.

Others bake them in the oven at a low temperature for six hours. But such methods are not for the true conker player. No world-champion conker has ever been produced by short cuts . . .

"The best conker I ever had was a conker 109, and I can still remember that frosty morning in the school playground when my one-o-nine was finally shattered by Perkins's conker 74 in an epic contest that lasted over half an hour. After it, I felt even more shattered than my conker!"

Roald Dahl's ADVENTURES

When Roald was sixteen, he decided to go off on his own to holiday in France. He crossed the Channel from Dover to Calais with £24 in his pocket (a lot of money in 1933). Roald wanted to see the Mediterranean Sea, so he took the train first to Paris, then on to Marseilles where he got on a bus that went all the way along the coastal road towards Monte Carlo. He finished up at a place called St. Jean Cap Ferrat and stayed there for ten days,

wandering around
by himself and
doing whatever he
wanted. It was his
first taste of absolute
freedom – and what
it was like to be a
grown-up.

He traveled
back home the
same way but
by the time he reached Dover, he had
absolutely no money left. Luckily a fellow
passenger gave him ten shillings for his
tram fare home. Roald never forgot this
kindness and generosity.

When Roald was seventeen he signed up
to go to Newfoundland, Canada, with

"The Public Schools' Exploring Society."
Together with thirty other boys, he spent
three weeks trudging over a desolate
landscape with an enormous rucksack.
It weighed so much that he needed
someone to help him hoist it on to his
back every morning. The boys lived on
pemmican (strips of pressed meat, fat and
berries) and lentils, and they experimented
with eating boiled lichen and reindeer
moss because they were so hungry. It was
a genuine adventure and left Roald fit and
ready for
anything!

Mr. Wonka's Chocolate Factory Recipes

Butterscotch

You will need:

Large saucepan
Large jug
Whisk
Plastic wrap

4 tsp butter
4 tsp superfine sugar
2 tsp honey
2 tsp corn syrup
2 ½ cups fat-free milk
⅓ cup natural yogurt

Makes approx 3–4 mugs

How to make:

1 In a saucepan, over a low heat, melt together the butter, sugar, honey, and corn syrup, stirring all the time until the sugar has dissolved (about ten minutes). Add a little milk to the pan, then transfer to a jug.

2 Whisk in a little more milk, approximately 3 tablespoons, followed by all of the yogurt.

3 Whisk in the remaining milk.

4 Cover with plastic wrap. Chill before serving.

Please ask a grown-up to help you when you are handling anything hot.

Roald Dahl's October

"This, like September, is a lovely month, mild and misty and smelling of ripe apples. We have a small orchard at the back of our house . . . there was so much fruit every autumn that I told all the children in the village they could come in at any time and ask to borrow a ladder and pick what they wanted. They came in droves . . .

"During October swarms of migrant birds cross the North Sea from Scandinavia to our

shores. Some, like starlings and blackbirds
and thrushes and rooks and jackdaws,
will stay here for the winter. Others, like the
skylarks and goldcrests and finches, will rest
before going on south to spend the winter
in Africa . . .

"At this time of year our hedges are covered with old man's beard and woody nightshade. Hips and haws make splashes of crimson everywhere. In the grassy banks on either side, an enormous number of different wild flowers and ferns grow. On weekends I see groups of enthusiastic botanists from London hunting for rare specimens. They walk slowly up the lane peering into the banks and calling to one another when they find something interesting. I like these people. I like enthusiasts of any kind. "

Charlie's Quiz

 How many new kinds of chocolate bar has Mr. Willy Wonka invented?

 What did Prince Pondicherry ask Willy Wonka to do?

 How do the chocolates and sweets come out of Mr. Wonka's factory?

4 *Why does Violet Beauregarde turn into a gigantic blueberry?*

5 How many Golden Tickets are there altogether?

6 *Who finds the second Golden Ticket?*

7 What does Violet Beauregarde do all day?

8 *What does Mike Teavee like doing best?*

9　In what kind of chocolate bar does Charlie find his Golden Ticket?

10　*What sort of coat does Willy Wonka wear?*

11　Where are the most important rooms in Willy Wonka's factory?

12　*How is the chocolate mixed?*

13　What happens to Augustus Gloop?

14　*What is Willy Wonka's private yacht made from?*

15 Which is the most important room in the whole factory?

16 *Who pushes Veruca Salt down the rubbish chute?*

17 Why is the elevator so special?

18 *What happens when Willy Wonka presses the UP AND OUT button in the elevator?*

19 What does Mike Teavee look like when he leaves the factory?

20 *What present does Willy Wonka decide to give Charlie?*

Turn to page 118 for the answers –
if you really have to!

Roald Dahl's
November

❝November is the middle of what we used
to call the Christmas term. I had my first
Christmas term away from home when I was
eight years old. And it is also the month of
fireworks and Guy Fawkes. Oh, how we used
to look forward to the fifth of November at
boarding school . . . We had jackie jumpers,
Roman candles, crack-bangers, fire-
serpents, big bombers, rockets and
golden rain!

"There is a badger's earth in the wood above our house, and this month the badgers are busy digging their deep winter quarters and lining them with dry leaves for warmth. Before November is out, they will have blocked up the entrances to their holes and will sleep the winter through. Like the badgers, the grass snakes are all starting to hibernate, but they are not as domesticated as the badgers. They have no real homes and simply hide themselves among the twisted tree roots underneath the hedges, and quite often they will coil themselves around each other for comfort. For many small animals, the approach of winter means the time to go to sleep until spring arrives again. It would make life a lot more comfortable if we could do the same!"

Roald Dahl's Secret Writing Tips

"The job of a children's writer is to try to write a book that is so exciting and fast and wonderful that the child falls in love with it."

Have you got what it takes to be an author? You might well have – it's just that you don't know it yet!

Believe it or not, Roald Dahl only found out he could write by accident. At the age of twenty-six he was "discovered" by C. S. Forester, author of the Captain Horatio Hornblower stories. From that moment, he never stopped writing.

But it's not easy. These are the qualities Roald Dahl suggested you will need if you are going to become a writer:

1. "You should have a lively imagination.
2. You should be able to write well. By that I mean you should be able to make a scene come alive in the reader's mind.

3 You must have stamina. In other words, you must be able to stick to what you are doing and never give up.

4 You must be a perfectionist. That means you must never be satisfied with what you have written until you have rewritten it again and again, making it as good as you possibly can.

5 You must have strong self-discipline.

6 It helps a lot if you have a keen sense of humour.

7 You must have a degree of humility. The writer who thinks that his work is marvelous is heading for trouble."

Point 4 is crucial. Roald Dahl spent many months writing *Charlie and the Chocolate Factory* and, as you know, there was a first draft, then a second, then a third, and so on. Some bits were added in, other bits taken out. With each rewrite, the story would get better and better.

Roald Dahl's December

"One Christmas, when I was about nine or ten, I had been given a fine Meccano set as my main present, and I decided I would make a device that was capable of 'bombing' from the air the pedestrians using the public footpath across our land.

"Briefly my plan was as follows: I would stretch a wire all the way from the high roof of our house to the old garage on the other side of the footpath. Then I would construct from my Meccano a machine that would hang from the wire by a grooved wheel and this machine would hopefully run down the wire at great speed dropping its bombs on the unwary walkers underneath.

"Next morning, filled with the enthusiasm that grips all great inventors, I climbed on to the roof of our house by the skylight and wrapped one end of the long roll of wire around a chimney. I threw the rest of the wire into the garden below and went back down myself through the skylight. I carried the wire across the garden, over the fence, across the footpath, over the next fence and into our land on the other side. I now pulled the wire very tight and fixed it with a big nail to the top of the door of the old garage. So far so good.

"Next I set about constructing from the
Meccano my bombing machine, or chariot
as I called it. I put the wheel at the top, and
then running down from the wheel I made a
strong column about three feet long (a meter).
At the lower end of this column, I fixed two
arms that projected outwards at right angles,
one on either side, and along these arms
I suspended five empty Heinz soup tins.
The whole thing looked something like this:

". . . I filled all the soup tins with water.
I lay flat on the roof waiting for a victim.
Soon two ladies dressed in tweed skirts
and jackets and each wearing a hat, came
strolling up the path with a revolting little
Pekinese dog on a lead. I knew I had to time
this carefully, so when they were very nearly
but not quite directly under the wire, I let
my chariot go. Down she went, making a
wonderful screeching-humming noise as
the metal wheel ran down the wire and the
string ran through my fingers at great speed.
Bombing from a height is never easy. I had
to guess when my chariot was directly over
the target, and when that moment came,
I jerked the string. The chariot stopped dead
and the tins swung upside down and all the
water tipped out. The ladies, who had halted

and looked up on hearing the rushing noise
of my chariot overhead, caught the cascade of
water full in their faces. It was tremendous.
A bulls-eye first time. The women screamed.
I lay flat on the roof so as not to be seen,
peering over the edge, and I saw the women
shouting and waving their arms. Then they
came marching straight into our garden
through the gate at the back and crossed the
garden and hammered on the door. I nipped
down smartly through the skylight and did
a bunk.

"Later on my mother fixed me with a
steely eye and told me she was confiscating
my Meccano set for the rest of the holidays.
But for days afterwards I experienced the
pleasant warm glow that comes to all of us
when we have brought off a major triumph!"

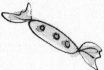

Charlie's Chocolate Shop

At one time, *Charlie and the Chocolate Factory* was going to end very differently! This was the ending in an earlier version:

The shop has been finished now, and it is the most beautiful chocolate shop in the world. It occupies a whole block in the center of the city, and it is nine storeys high.

Inside it, there are moving staircases and
elevators to take the customers up and
down, and no less than one hundred ladies,
all dressed in spotless gold and chocolate
uniforms, are there to serve behind the

counters. They will sell you anything you want from a single little blue bird's egg with a tiny sugary bird inside it to a life-size chocolate elephant with huge curvy tusks and a chocolate elephant driver sitting on its back.

And Charlie Bucket, coming home from school in the evenings, nearly always brings along with him about twenty or thirty of his friends and tells them that they can choose anything they want – for free.

"It's my shop," he says. "Just help yourselves."

And so they do.

Isn't it amazing how much a book can change before it is published?

Secrets are everywhere.
If you keep looking hard enough,
you might just find something new and
magical that has never been seen before.
Who knows? One day you may even
discover the secret of what it takes
to become as great a writer
as Roald Dahl!

Answers to Charlie's Quiz

1 More than two hundred
2 Build him a chocolate palace
3 Through a special trap door in the wall
4 Because she chews a piece of the three-course-dinner chewing-gum
5 Five
6 Veruca Salt
7 She chews gum
8 Watching television
9 A Whipple-Scrumptious Fudgemallow Delight
10 A tailcoat made of plum-colored velvet
11 Underground
12 By waterfall
13 He falls into the chocolate river and gets sucked up a pipe into the strawberry-flavored chocolate-coated fudge room
14 An enormous hollowed-out boiled sweet
15 The Inventing Room
16 The squirrels
17 It can go in any direction, and visit any room in the factory
18 The elevator flies out through the roof of the factory
19 About ten feet tall and thin as a wire
20 The whole chocolate factory

THERE'S MORE TO ROALD DAHL
THAN GREAT STORIES...

Did you know that 10% of author royalties* from this book go to help the work of the Roald Dahl charities?

Roald Dahl's Marvellous Children's Charity exists to make life better for seriously ill children because it believes that every child has the right to a marvellous life.

This marvellous charity helps thousands of children each year living with serious conditions of the blood and the brain – causes important to Roald Dahl in his lifetime – whether by providing nurses, equipment or toys for today's children in the UK, or helping tomorrow's children everywhere through pioneering research.

Can you do something marvellous to help others?
Find out how at **www.marvellouschildrenscharity.org**

The Roald Dahl Museum and Story Centre, based in Great Missenden just outside London, is in the Buckinghamshire village where Roald Dahl lived and wrote. At the heart of the Museum, created to inspire a love of reading and writing, is his unique archive of letters and manuscripts. As well as two fun-packed biographical galleries, the Museum boasts an interactive Story Centre. It is a place for the family, teachers and their pupils to explore the exciting world of creativity and literacy.
www.roalddahlmuseum.org

Roald Dahl's Marvellous Children's Charity is a registered charity no. 1137409

The Roald Dahl Museum and Story Centre is a registered charity no. 1085853

The Roald Dahl Charitable Trust is a registered charity that supports the work of RDMCC and RDMSC

* Donated royalties are net of commission